★ *GREAT SPORTS TEAMS* ★

THE MONTREAL

HOCKEY TEAM

David Aretha

Enslow Publishers, Inc.

44 Fadem Road   PO Box 38
Box 699   Aldershot
Springfield, NJ 07081 Hants GU12 6BP
USA   UK

Library of Congress Cataloging-in-Publication Data

Aretha, David.
    The Montreal Canadiens hockey team / David Aretha.
       p. cm. — (Great sports teams)
    Summary: A team history of the most successful franchise in professional
hockey, highlighting star players, coaches, and their many championship
seasons.
    Includes bibliographical references (p.) and index.
    ISBN 0-7660-1022-8
    1. Montreal Canadiens (Hockey team)—History—Juvenile literature.
[1. Montreal Canadiens (Hockey team) 2. Hockey—History.] I. Title. II. Series.
GV848.M6A74 1998
796.962′64′0971428—dc21   97-21308
                                                  CIP
                                                    AC

Printed in the United States of America

10 9 8 7 6 5 4 3 2 1

Illustration Credits: AP/Wide World Photos, pp. 4, 7, 8, 10, 13, 14, 16,
19, 20, 22, 25, 26, 28, 31, 32, 34, 37, 38.

Cover Illustration: AP/Wide World Photos.

CONTENTS

*M*aurice "Rocket" Richard terrorized NHL goalies for 18 seasons.

ROCKET FUEL

A hushed murmur ran through the crowd at the Montreal Forum. Maurice "Rocket" Richard, the dynamic goal-scorer and beloved hero of French Canada, lay flat on the ice. He was motionless, perhaps unconscious. Blood oozed from his forehead.

The Rocket Is Grounded

The players for the Montreal Canadiens and Boston Bruins skated around, nervous and shaken. Though the stakes of this game were high—it was the seventh game of the 1952 Stanley Cup semifinals—players had other things on their minds. The Rocket was down; a legend had fallen.

Moments earlier Richard had been storming into the Boston zone when defenseman Leo Labine went after him. Labine, using his knee and stick, knocked Richard off his feet. The Rocket fell face first, slamming the ice with his forehead. He lay still, blood streaking past his left eye.

Smelling salts finally brought Richard to his senses. However, he had to be helped to his feet and escorted to the dressing room. Canadiens fans, who loved Richard more than any other public figure, applauded their hero as he left the ice. Though it was only the second period, no one expected to see him again in this game—and maybe not until the next season.

In the locker room doctors went to work on Richard. They sewed his wound with six stitches and then bandaged it. His doctors said he was in a partial coma.[1] Somehow, the gritty Richard returned to the bench for the third period. Yet the Rocket was so groggy that he couldn't see the numbers on the score-board. It was all a blur.

An Amazing Return

Of course, Coach Dick Irvin didn't want to have to use Richard. Yet the score remained gridlocked at 1–1, and the loser would go home for the spring and summer. With four minutes to go, Richard—one of the toughest men ever to lace up skates—hopped onto the ice. Fans were thrilled just to see the Rocket on his feet.

Richard, still dazed, soon grabbed a loose puck in his own end. He drove around Boston's Woody Dumart and charged up the ice. Now in a mad rush, Richard dashed to center and then cut to the right, eluding opponents like a running back dodges defenders.

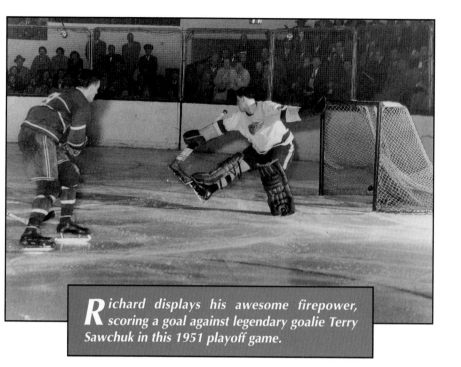

*R*ichard displays his awesome firepower, scoring a goal against legendary goalie Terry Sawchuk in this 1951 playoff game.

Boston defenseman Bill Quackenbush seemed to cut off Richard's path. Yet the Rocket—his eyes all lit up—whizzed past Quackenbush. Richard still seemed too far to the right to sneak a shot past goalie Sugar Jim Henry. Players call it the "impossible angle." But in a flickering instant, Richard—using only his right hand—drilled a shot past Henry and into the back of the net.

Richard had shocked everyone in the arena—including Henry. "One moment I was facing him, waiting for the shot," Henry said. "The next he had whizzed by and the puck was in the net."[2]

For the next four minutes, the Montreal fans stood on their feet, applauding their favorite son. In place of confetti, they showered the ice with programs, popcorn

Rocket Fuel

Legendary scorer Jean Beliveau waves to the throngs of fans who lined the streets of Montreal to honor the winners of the 1956 Stanley Cup.

boxes, and other celebratory debris.[3] "It was the greatest goal in NHL history," said Boston coach Lynn Patrick. "A truck wouldn't have stopped Richard on that play."[4]

What made the goal so stunning was the state Richard was in. The man was partially unconscious. "I was dizzy," he said. "I wasn't sure if I was skating toward their goal or our goal."[5]

The Canadiens hung on to win the game 2–1. Henry and Richard greeted each other after the game. Henry, looking beaten and beleaguered, shook hands with Richard, who had blood streaming down the left side of his face.

***

A Beautiful Home

It seems appropriate that the greatest goal ever scored occurred in the Montreal Forum, the site of more hockey drama than any other arena. In seventy-three years of National Hockey League (NHL) play, Forum fans cheered the game's greatest skaters (Howie Morenz, Guy Lafleur), hardest shooters (Richard, Boom Boom Geoffrion), and its most spectacular puck-stoppers (Jacques Plante, Patrick Roy).

Moreover, Montreal fans have seen more Stanley Cup drama than any other group. Thirty-two times the Canadiens, also known as the Habs (short for *Les Habitants*), have advanced to the Cup Finals. Twenty-four times they have hoisted Lord Stanley's mug. Canadiens fans are the proudest in North America. Thanks to heroes such as Richard, they also have the richest memories.

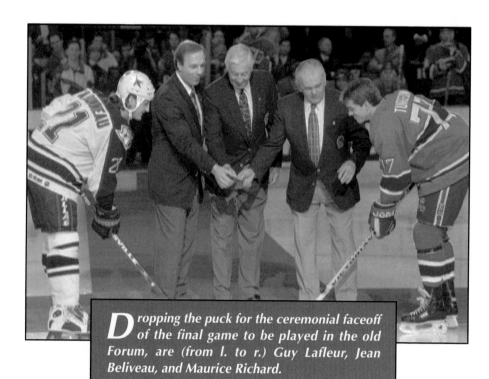

*D*ropping the puck for the ceremonial faceoff of the final game to be played in the old Forum, are (from l. to r.) Guy Lafleur, Jean Beliveau, and Maurice Richard.

TEAM HISTORY

They cheered for the last time. In the final game ever at the Montreal Forum, on March 11, 1996, Canadiens fans stood as one. Roused with memories and emotion, they applauded, hooted, hollered, and even shed a few tears. Above them, twenty-four Stanley Cup banners hung in the rafters. Below, dozens of returning Canadiens stars shivered in the fans' applause.

Rocket Richard alone received a ten-minute standing ovation. It brought the grizzled seventy-four-year-old to tears. "They didn't want to stop cheering for him," said Montreal captain Pierre Turgeon.[1]

For seventy-two years devoted fans had flocked to this hockey shrine. For them, the Canadiens represented all that was great about French Canada: grace and elegance; artistry and style; spirit and pride.

Said retired player Jim Roberts, "The Canadiens are not Montreal's team, not Quebec's team. They are Canada's team. The team is as cosmopolitan as the city."[2]

The Montreal Canadiens date back to 1909, when J. Ambrose O'Brien formed the club. The French-speaking team competed in the National Hockey Association, a precursor to the NHL. They skated at the outdoor Jubilee rink, with fans trudging to games in zero-degree weather.

Even then Canadiens players dressed in red, white, and blue. Early star Jack Laviolette possessed the speed and grace that would become a team trademark. The Canadiens won one Stanley Cup, in 1916, before joining the newly formed NHL a year later.

Joining the NHL

Joe Malone starred on the 1917–18 Canadiens, netting a staggering 44 goals in just 20 games. The next decade, however, would be marked more by tragedy than success. The Canadiens reached the Stanley Cup series, against the Seattle Metropolitans, in 1919. However, the dreaded Spanish influenza gripped the Montrealers. Canadiens star "Bad Joe" Hall died from the virus, and the Stanley Cup Finals were canceled. In 1926, Montreal's brilliant puck-stopper, Georges Vezina, died of tuberculosis.

A new era dawned in 1924, when the fabulous Montreal Forum opened for play. Another NHL team, the English community's Montreal Maroons, shared the rink with the Canadiens. Yet the Maroons couldn't

Montreal captain Yvan Cournoyer celebrates the 1976 Stanley Cup victory. The Canadiens have won more championships than any other major professional sports team in history.

match the flair of their counterparts. Spurred by speedy, dazzling Howie Morenz, the Canadiens became known as the "Flying Frenchmen." They captured the Stanley Cup in 1924, 1930, and 1931.

Canada was gripped by the Great Depression in the 1930s, and Montreal hockey went down with it. Morenz died of heart failure in 1937. The Maroons, struggling financially, folded in 1938. The Canadiens stayed afloat, but sagged in the standings.

Enter the Rocket. In 1943–44 Canadiens coach Dick Irvin put a young goal-scoring dynamo, Maurice "Rocket" Richard, on a line with Toe Blake and Elmer Lach. They called it the "Punch Line," and the trio bedazzled opposing goalies with their scoring magic.

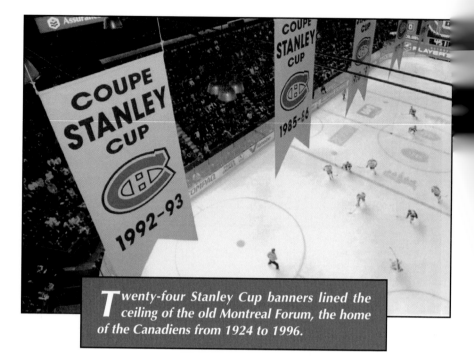

*T*wenty-four Stanley Cup banners lined the ceiling of the old Montreal Forum, the home of the Canadiens from 1924 to 1996.

The Canadiens record from 1943–46 was 104–30–16. Twice they hoisted Lord Stanley's cup.

From 1943–79 the Canadiens reigned as the most enduring dynasty in hockey history. Two general managers, Frank Selke and then Sam Pollack, kept the engine running. Coaches Irvin, Blake, and Scotty Bowman steered the ship. These men signed the best talent, made the shrewdest trades, and schooled their players in Canadiens-style hockey. Slick skating and crisp passing drew praise. Bullying and hot-dogging did not.

Over the years the Canadiens have skated out star after star. Elegant Jean Beliveau and power-shooting Bernie "Boom Boom" Geoffrion helped Montreal win five straight Cups from 1956–60. Pint-sized playmakers Henri Richard (Maurice's little brother) and Yvan "the

Roadrunner" Cournoyer hoisted six Cups from 1964–73. Guy Lafleur, Beliveau's heir apparent, sparked Montreal to four straight titles from 1976–79. Chants of "Guy, Guy, Guy" reverberated throughout the rink.

Spectacular goaltending and stringent defense were other Canadiens hallmarks. Ambidextrous Bill Durnan, Jacques "The Roamer" Plante, and Ken Dryden won a combined seventeen Vezina Trophies as the league's premier goalies. Well-schooled defensemen such as Doug Harvey and Larry Robinson kept opposing skaters in line. For fifty-one years in a row (1943–94), Montreal's goals-against average (GAA) was below the league average.

The Recent Champions

Though Montreal's offense has waned since the early 1980s, the defense and goaltending have not. Awe-inspiring netminding by Patrick Roy led to Stanley Cups in 1986 and 1993.

The Canadiens have a motto: "To you, with fallen hands, we throw the torch, be yours to hold it high." In the final game at the Forum, all living Canadiens captains passed a torch to one another. Butch Bouchard carried it from the dressing room to the ice, handing it to Rocket Richard. He passed it to Beliveau, who gave it to Henri Richard. Down the line it went, to active captain Turgeon, who skated off the ice.

Days later the Canadiens moved to the Molson Centre. With them they took the twenty-four Stanley Cup banners—as well as eighty-seven years' worth of memories.

*K*nown as the "Babe Ruth of hockey," Howie Morenz led the Canadiens to three Stanley Cups in the 1920s and 1930s.

SUPER SKATERS

Through the decades many great players have laced up their skates for the Montreal Canadiens. Each of these players has led the Canadiens to multiple Stanley Cup championships.

Howie Morenz

So spectacular was Howie Morenz that one nickname wasn't enough. Fans called him the "Stratford Streak," the "Canadien Comet," and the "Babe Ruth of hockey."

Fans in the 1920s rushed to arenas to see the fastest man on skates. "When Howie skates full speed," said an opponent, "everyone else on the ice seems to be skating backward."[1] Morenz shot so hard that he once knocked a goalie on his back.[2] Ferocious on the ice, Morenz enjoyed life off of it, often singing and playing the ukulele.

Morenz played twelve seasons with Montreal, winning three Stanley Cups and three Hart Trophies as league Most Valuable Player (MVP). When he died unexpectedly at age thirty-four, 25,000 mourners paid their respects.

Maurice "Rocket" Richard

Goalie Glenn Hall remembered Maurice "Rocket" Richard: "When he came flying toward you with the puck on his stick, his eyes were all lit up, flashing and gleaming like a pinball machine. It was terrifying."[3]

The right wing on Montreal's "Punch Line," Richard abused goalies from 1942–60. Said referee Bill Chadwick, "I saw him carry defensemen on his back right up to the goalmouth and score."[4] Richard would launch his rocket shot or—because he was ambidextrous—fool goalies with a last-second back-hander.

Richard was the first NHL player to score five goals in a playoff game, 50 goals in a season (1944–45), and 500 in a career. Rocket was beloved more than any other Canadiens player. When the league president suspended him in 1955, the city rioted in revolt.

Jacques Plante

After Andy Bathgate's slap shot bloodied his face in a 1959 game, Montreal goalie Jacques Plante decided to wear a face mask. He thus became the first NHL goalie to regularly do so. A true innovator, "Jacques the Roamer" was also the first wandering netminder, charging out of the crease to grab loose pucks.

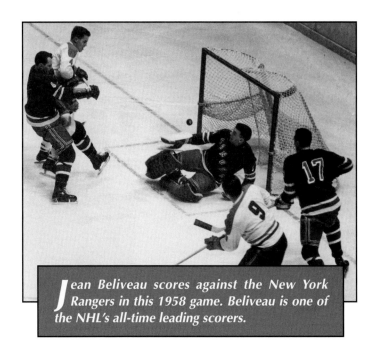

Jean Beliveau scores against the New York Rangers in this 1958 game. Beliveau is one of the NHL's all-time leading scorers.

The Canadiens signed the wandering goalie in 1953. During the next ten years, Plante won six Vezina Trophies (as the league's best goalie) and led Montreal to five straight Stanley Cups (1956–60). "For five years, Jacques was the greatest goalie the league has ever seen," said his coach, Toe Blake.[5] His 424 victories rank second in NHL history.

Jean Beliveau

So elegant was Jean Beliveau that the press called him "Le Prince Royal du Hockey." "The playing of Beliveau," wrote Hugh MacLennan, "was poetry in action."[6]

Checking Jean Beliveau, said Bill Ezinicki, "was like running into the side of a big oak tree."[7] However, the classy handsome Beliveau played with grace and

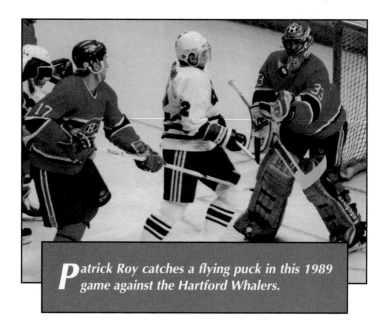

*P*atrick Roy catches a flying puck in this 1989 game against the Hartford Whalers.

finesse. "His stick-handling ability," wrote Stan Fischler, "suggested that he had an invisible string linking the puck to his stick blade."[8] Beliveau could also score in bunches. On November 5, 1955, he netted three goals in 44 seconds.

In his career, Beliveau led Montreal to an amazing ten Stanley Cups. He retired with 507 goals and 1,219 points, establishing NHL records for a center. On "Jean Beliveau Night" in 1971, the Prime Minister of Canada, Pierre Trudeau, personally honored Le Prince. "Beliveau," stated Trudeau, "has given new prestige to hockey."[9]

Guy Lafleur

In French, Guy Lafleur's last name means "the flower." The name was appropriate since Lafleur was such a beautiful player to watch.

Fans first took notice of Lafleur in 1970–71, when he scored 130 goals in junior hockey. Lafleur soon became one of Montreal's great "Flying Frenchmen." "In practice, he would make moves that left you speechless," said teammate Ken Dryden.[10]

From 1974–79, Lafleur accomplished the following: He scored fifty or more goals in six straight seasons. He won three scoring titles and two Hart Trophies as league MVP. And he led Montreal to four straight Stanley Cups (1976–79).

Lafleur finished his career in 1991 with 560 goals. He was, said teammate Gary Roberts, "the most exciting player I've ever seen."[11]

Patrick Roy

Roy in French means "king," and at times Montreal goalie Patrick Roy was just that.

In the 1986 playoffs Roy, just a twenty-year-old rookie, posted a minuscule 1.92 goals-against average and led the Canadiens to the Stanley Cup. In the 1993 playoffs Roy won 10 consecutive overtime games on the way to another Cup. "He was just outstanding," beamed his coach, Jacques Demers. "Sensational. Dominating."[12]

Roy did his best work on his knees, sprawling and snaring pucks with his catlike quickness. In ten years with Montreal, Roy won two Vezina Trophies as the league's best goalie and played in six All-Star Games. He also puck-stopped Colorado to a Stanley Cup in 1996, recording a triple-overtime shutout in the finale.

*D*ick Irvin coached Montreal to three Stanley Cups. When he retired in 1956, Irvin held the record for most wins with 790. Scotty Bowman now holds the record.

FRONT OFFICE HEROES

There have been many great hockey minds in charge of the Canadiens. Coaches such as Dick Irvin, Toe Blake, and Scotty Bowman led their teams to glory. The shrewd front office minds of Frank Selke and Sam Pollack stocked the organization with the finest talent.

Dick Irvin

He may have looked conservative in his dark suits and fedora hats. In reality, Dick Irvin was colorfully innovative.

Prior to World War II, NHL hockey had been a plodding, defensive-oriented game. Irvin broke the mold. His speedy, go-for-broke teams of 1943–44 and 1944–45 scored goals by the bunches and were a combined 76–13–11. In the 1953 playoffs Irvin unveiled goalie Jacques Plante, an exotic rookie who wandered way out of the goal crease. Plante led Montreal to the Stanley Cup.

As a player, Irvin had been a sharp-shooting winger in the 1910s and 1920s. He coached an NHL-record 26 seasons, mostly with Toronto (1931–40) and Montreal (1940–55). Irvin copped three Cups with the Canadiens (1944, 1946, and 1953) and set a coaching record with 690 victories.

Frank Selke

Frank Selke didn't create the Montreal juggernaut. He just kept the engine running—for sixteen years.

An electrician by trade, Selke was also a talented administrator with the Toronto Maple Leafs. He became the Canadiens' manager in 1946—but he didn't like what he saw. "I told [the Montreal owners] that no other team could match their top six players," Selke said. "But there were no reserves, no farm system."[1]

So Selke, a patient and well-organized man, created a large, efficient farm system. Over the years, brilliant stars rose through the ranks. Jean Beliveau, Boom Boom Geoffrion, Dickie Moore, Doug Harvey, and Jacques Plante were among the steady stream of All-Stars. When Selke retired in 1962, the Canadiens had hoisted six Stanley Cups.

So esteemed was Selke that the NHL honors his name with an annual award. Each year the league's best defensive forward receives the Frank Selke Trophy.

*H*ector *"Toe" Blake won eight Stanley Cups, more than any other coach in NHL history. Blake is flanked by (from l. to r.) Jacques Plante, Maurice Richard, and Bernie Geoffrion.*

Hector "Toe" Blake

When the Canadiens needed a new coach in 1955, they searched for a special man. They needed a smart hockey guy with championship experience. They needed a leader who commanded the respect of veteran stars Jean Beliveau and Bernie Geoffrion. And they needed a psychologist who could handle the delicate psyche of rambunctious superstar Maurice Richard. They needed Hector "Toe" Blake, and they got him. In his first five years as coach Blake won five Stanley Cups.

From 1943–48, Blake had skated on Montreal's famed "Punch Line" with Richard and Elmer Lach. Known as "Old Lamplighter," Blake led the NHL in scoring in 1938–39.

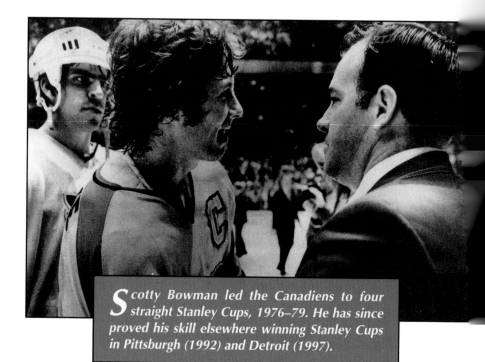

S cotty Bowman led the Canadiens to four straight Stanley Cups, 1976–79. He has since proved his skill elsewhere winning Stanley Cups in Pittsburgh (1992) and Detroit (1997).

As a coach, Blake was supreme dictator. He would bench players who slacked off and slam locker room doors to get his team's attention. Yet he was fair. "Toe doesn't humiliate you," said goalie Gump Worsley, "or mouth off to the press."[2] Blake was also one of the boys, socializing with his players after games. Blake won three more Stanley Cups (1964, 1965, and 1968) before retiring.

Sam Pollack

In fourteen years as GM, Sam Pollack won nine Stanley Cups. He was never afraid to shake things up either. Though Montreal won the Cup in 1968 and 1969, Pollack dismantled the team. He traded away mainstays Bobby Rousseau, Ralph Backstrom, and others. In return he got draft picks; he had eleven first-round choices from 1969–72. Pollack used the 1971 pick to draft the great Guy Lafleur. Also in 1971 Pollack promoted rookie goalie Ken Dryden. Though this was a "rebuilding" year, the Canadiens won the Cup.

When Pollack's draft picks (Lafleur, Steve Shutt, and Bob Gainey, etc.) matured, a new Canadiens dynasty was born. Pollack retired as GM in 1978. He became an expert in investments, making shrewd deals.

Scotty Bowman

A stern, tough taskmaster, Scotty Bowman became the winningest coach in NHL history. "The players hated Scotty 364 days a year," wrote Al Strachan. "On the other day, they cashed their Stanley Cup cheques."[3]

Coach Bowman succeeded with other NHL teams—St. Louis, Buffalo, Pittsburgh, Detroit. Yet it was with Montreal that he achieved ultimate success. Named Canadiens coach in 1971, Bowman won Stanley Cups in 1973, 1976, 1978, and 1979. His 1975–76 team (60–8–12) has been called the greatest of all time.

The son of a blacksmith, Bowman was a no-frills guy. He seldom smiled and never chummed with his players. He taught them well, pushed them hard, and expected wins. During games he was also a master strategist. "I've seen Bowman outcoach people," said NHL coach Pierre Maguire. "Just eat them up."[4]

Bowman's mother once said, "If you like the game, Scott, why lose at it?"[5] Bowman took that to heart, winning his 1,000th NHL game with Detroit in 1994.

*T*wenty-one-year old Maurice Richard joined the Canadiens during the 1942–43 season, marking the beginning of one of the greatest dynasties in hockey history.

FANTASTIC SEASONS

The Montreal Canadiens have had more championship seasons than any other major sports franchise. Many of their banner years came during periods when the Canadiens dominated the league for more than three years at a time.

1927-32

They dipped, darted, danced, and pranced. They were the "Flying Frenchmen," the most exciting team that hockey had ever seen. From 1927–28 through 1931–32, these Canadiens had the best record in the league three times. The other two years, 1929–30 and 1930–31, they won the Stanley Cup.

Howie Morenz, Johnny Gagnon, and Aurel Joliat comprised the marquee line. With his burning speed and relentless determination, Morenz led the NHL in scoring in 1927–28 and 1930–31. Gagnon, nicknamed

"Black Cat," was a quick, nimble, puck-handling wizard. As for "Tiny" Joliat, "he transported the world of ballet to the hockey arena."[1] In goal stood the incomparable George Hainsworth. In 1928–29, Hainsworth allowed just 43 goals in 44 games!

In the 1931 Finals the Canadiens came from behind to defeat Chicago. When Morenz scored the clinching goal, the Montreal fans littered the ice with coins, programs, and galoshes.[2] Only the Flying Frenchmen could rouse fans into such a frenzy.

1943-46

Which was the most dominating team in NHL history? Many historians cast their votes for the 1943–46 Canadiens. Coach Dick Irvin's boys rang up records of 38–5–7, 38–8–4, and 28–17–5. Twice they won Lord Stanley's cup.

The fabled "Punch Line" poured in the goals. Center Elmer Lach—fast as a rabbit, tough as a bulldog—earned league MVP honors in 1944–45. That same year, at right wing, master blaster Maurice Richard netted an NHL record 50 goals. As for left wing Toe Blake: "He was the team's spark plug," said hockey historian William Roche, "and its anchor."[3] All-Star Butch Bouchard led the stingiest defense in the league. In goal, ambidextrous Bill Durnan stopped pucks with both hands.

Though Toronto upset Montreal in the 1945 play-offs, the Canadiens blew through the postseason in 1944 and 1946. Each year they won eight of nine playoff

*B*ernie *"Boom Boom" Geoffrion was one of many great Canadiens players. He led the league in scoring in 1954–55.*

games. Their 11–0 humiliation of Chicago in a 1944 playoff game illustrated their superiority.

1956-60

The Canadiens didn't just win five straight Stanley Cups from 1956–60. They utterly dominated their competition. In 49 playoff games, Montreal won 40 times. Boston goalie Don Simmons was beaten so badly in a 1957 Finals game that "my back's sunburned from all those red lights."[4]

The following Canadiens finished among the NHL's top five scorers at one time or another: right wings Maurice Richard and Bernie Geoffrion, centers Jean Beliveau and Henri Richard, and left wings Dickie

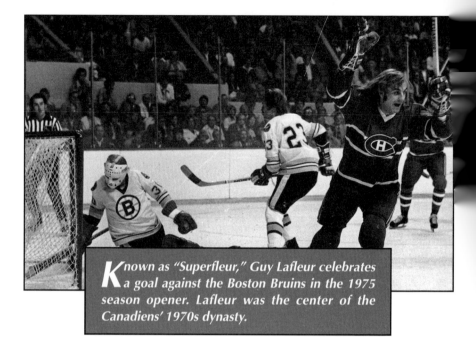

Known as "Superfleur," Guy Lafleur celebrates a goal against the Boston Bruins in the 1975 season opener. Lafleur was the center of the Canadiens' 1970s dynasty.

Moore and Bert Olmstead. Moreover, the Canadiens perennially iced the best defense. Backliner Doug Harvey and goalie Jacques Plante reigned supreme.

In their ten playoff series, Montreal beat New York, Boston, Detroit, Chicago, and Toronto twice each. After awhile, it got to be old hat. "When you win the final series in four games," said Harvey, "there's just not much to get excited about."[5]

1964-69

It's hard to replace a legend, let alone four. Without Rocket Richard, Jacques Plante, Doug Harvey, and Bernie Geoffrion, the 1960s Canadiens were mere mortals. That they won four Stanley Cups—in 1965, 1966, 1968, and 1969—is a tribute to their guts and savvy.

Team leader Jean Beliveau led a competent, but not overwhelming Montreal offense. Jacques Laperriere and J. C. Tremblay powered the tough defense. In goal, Gump Worsley, Charlie Hodge, and Rogie Vachon did themselves proud.

Of course, none of Montreal's Stanley Cup runs was easy. Twice the Canadiens survived seven-game wars—against Chicago (1965 Finals) and Boston (1969 semis). Montreal coach Toe Blake retired in 1968. "I can't stand the pressure anymore," he said.[6]

1975-79

Though one of the league's premier teams in the early 1970s, Montreal entered a league of its own in 1975. From 1975–76 through 1978–79, the Canadiens won all four Stanley Cups. Their records were—brace yourself—58–11–11, 60–8–12, 59–10–11, and 52–17–11.

Coach Scotty Bowman's team relied on speed, skill, and finesse—as well as team unity. "We were a family," said two-time league MVP Guy Lafleur. "We used to stick more together with the players than with our wives."[7]

Jacques Lemaire centered a line with Lafleur and Steve Shutt, the NHL's two deadliest scorers. Defensively, All-Stars Larry Robinson, Serge Savard, and Guy Lapointe policed their own end. Rangy netminder Ken Dryden sealed the goal. In 1976–77 the Canadiens outscored opponents 387–171.

"The 1975–76 and 1976–77 Canadiens teams," said Boston coach Don Cherry, "may have been the best ever in the NHL."[8]

*M*ark Recchi celebrates after a Canadiens'
goal. A hard worker, Recchi is one of the
top scorers on Montreal's current team.

PRESENT AND FUTURE

t 10:30 of sudden death, Montreal's Vince Damphousse knocked in a power-play goal against Quebec goalie Ron Hextall. It gave the Canadiens a 2–1 playoff victory, and it triggered the most spectacular Stanley Cup joyride in NHL history. During the 1993 playoffs the Canadiens repeatedly turned sudden-death overtime (OT) into automatic victory.

Montreal's Kirk Muller netted another OT winner in Game 5 of the opening-round Quebec series. Against the Buffalo Sabres in Round 2, Montreal swept the series, winning the last three games in the extra session. When the chips were down, no one could dent Canadiens goalie Patrick Roy. "How do you spell mystique?" asked Quebec coach Pierre Page. "R-O-Y."[1]

In the Eastern Conference finals, Montreal shot down the New York Islanders in five games, winning

Games 2 and 3 in overtime. The magic continued in the Stanley Cup Finals against Wayne Gretzky's Los Angeles Kings. With fans waving the banner "INC-ROY-HAB-LE," Roy won Games 2, 3, and 4 in OT. He had thus won ten overtime games in ten attempts. In 96:39 of sudden death, he had stopped 65 of 65 shots.

"We didn't mind going into overtime," Roy said. "My concentration was at such a high level. My mind was right there. I felt fresh, like I could stop everything."[2] Montreal cruised to a 4–1 victory in Game 5, completing the team's magic carpet ride to the Stanley Cup.

A Rough Period

Unfortunately, Montreal fans have seen little magic since. Roy came down with appendicitis in the first round of the 1994 playoffs, and the Canadiens were doomed. In the strike-shortened season of 1994–95, Montreal won only three road games all year. The team failed to make the playoffs for the first time since 1970.

In 1995–96 Roy feuded with new coach Mario Tremblay. Roy was traded, and the Canadiens subsequently lost in the first round of the playoffs. No better news in 1996–97: a 31–36–15 record and a first-round playoff exit. The defense, which had been among the league's elite for fifty years, now ranked twenty-third in the NHL.

Despite the recent disappointments, the Canadiens have featured several standout performers.

V*ince Damphousse heads for the Colorado Avalanche's goal, which is guarded by former Canadiens great Patrick Roy.*

Damphousse possesses a deadly arsenal of wrist shots, snap shots, and slap shots. He has led Montreal in scoring three times, and he netted 40 goals in 1993–94. Veteran scoring great Pierre Turgeon enjoyed a brief fling in Montreal, scoring 38 goals and 96 points in 1995–96. Workaholic Mark Recchi, wringing every ounce of energy out of his five-foot ten-inch frame, mustered 80 points in 1996–97. On defense, Russian Vladimir Malakhov has wowed fans with his dazzling skating ability.

Home for the Future

Who will be the next great "Flying Frenchmen"? Montreal has a pair of candidates, although one's a

*F*ormer Finnish star Saku Koivu (11) celebrates a goal with teammates Marc Bureau (28), Patrice Brisbois (left), and Peter Popovic.

Finn and the other's a Russian. Finnish center Saku Koivu will thrill you offensively, then get back on defense and do the dirty work. He's just a little guy (five feet, nine inches), but so were Canadiens legends Yvan "the Roadrunner" Cournoyer and Henri "Pocket Rocket" Richard. Coaches rave about his intensity and commitment to the cause.

"I believe the best athletes are those who are most intense and most centered on their objective, which is to win," Koivu said. "As for the team, you have to be generous."

Montreal winger Valeri Bure is the brother of NHL All-Star Pavel Bure. Valeri Bure craves the puck, and when he gets it, he's not afraid to "let 'er rip." He once scored 68 goals in the Western Hockey League (1992–93).

A Return to Glory?

Despite Koivu and Bure, Montreal's talent is still middle-of-the-pack. The defense needs shoring up, and management is still searching for a successor to Roy. Throughout Quebec, fans debate whether the Canadiens will ever return to prominence.

Many fans remain optimistic. They hark back to Richard, Beliveau, and Lafleur. They refer to such intangibles as tradition and mystique. And they point to the twenty-four Stanley Cup banners hanging proudly above the ice. Will *les Canadiens* return to glory? Oh yes, they say. It's only a matter of time. . . .

STATISTICS

Team Record

The Canadiens NHL History

SEASONS	W	L	T	PCT	STANLEY CUPS
1917–18 to 1919–20	36	28	0	.563	None
1920–21 to 1929–30	176	123	39	.521	1924, 1930
1930–31 to 1939–40	188	212	76	.395	1931
1940–41 to 1949–50	268	192	86	.491	1944, 1946
1950–51 to 1959–60	365	212	123	.521	1953, 1956, 1957, 1958, 1959, 1960
1960–61 to 1969–70	382	205	129	.534	1965, 1966,1968, 1969
1970–71 to 1979–80	508	153	131	.641	1971, 1973, 1976 1977, 1978, 1979
1980–81 to 1989–90	429	260	111	.536	1986
1990–91 to 1996–97	258	208	74	.478	1993

The Canadiens Today

SEASON	W	L	T	PCT	COACH	DIVISION FINISH
1990–91	39	30	11	.488	Pat Burns	2nd Adams
1991–92	41	28	11	.513	Pat Burns	1st Adams
1992–93	48	30	6	.571	Jacques Demers	3rd Adams
1993–94	41	29	14	.488	Jacques Demers	3rd Northeast
1994–95	18	23	7	.375	Jacques Demers	6th Northeast
1995–96	40	32	10	.488	Jacques Demers Mario Tremblay	3rd Northeast
1996–97	31	36	15	.378	Mario Tremblay	4th Northeast

The Montreal Canadiens Hockey Team

Total History

W	L	T	PCT	STANLEY CUPS
2,610	1,593	769	.525	23*

*Montreal won a Stanley Cup in 1916 as a member of the National Hockey Association (NHA). The NHA disbanded in 1917 and the Canadiens joined the NHL.

W=Wins
L=Losses

T=Ties
PCT=Winning Percentage

STANLEY CUPS=Stanley Cups won

Championship Coaches

COACH	REGULAR SEASON			POST SEASON		STANLEY CUPS
	W	L	T	W	L	
Leo Danurand	55	42	5	10	4	1924
Cecil Hart	207	149	74	16	17	1930, 1931
Dick Irvin	431	313	152	62	53	1944, 1946, 1953
Toe Blake	500	255	159	82	37	1956, 1957, 1958, 1959, 1960, 1965, 1966, 1968,
Claude Ruel	172	82	51	18	9	1969
Al MacNeil	31	15	9	12	8	1971
Scotty Bowman	419	110	105	70	28	1973, 1976, 1977, 1978, 1979
Jean Perron	126	84	30	30	18	1986
Jacques Demers	107	86	27	19	8	1993

Statistics

Great Skaters

	CAREER STATISTICS					
PLAYER	SEA	YRS	GAMES	G	A	PTS
Jean Beliveau	1950–51, 1952–71	20	1,125	507	712	1,219
Bernie Geoffrion	1950–64	16	883	393	429	822
Doug Harvey	1947–61	19	1,113	88	452	540
Elmer Lach	1940–54	14	664	215	408	623
Guy Lafleur	1971–85	17	1,126	560	793	1,353
Joe Malone	1917–19, 1922–24	7	125	146	21	167
Howie Morenz	1923–34	14	550	270	197	467
Henri Richard	1955–75	20	1,256	358	688	1,046
Maurice Richard	1942–60	18	978	544	421	965
Larry Robinson	1972–89	20	1,384	208	750	958

SEA=Seasons with Canadiens   GAMES=Games Played   A=Assists
YRS=Years in the NHL   G=Goals   PTS=Points Scored

Great Goalies

	CAREER STATISTICS						
PLAYER	SEA	YRS	GAMES	MIN	GA	SH	GAA
Ken Dryden	1970–73, 1974–79	8	397	23,352	870	46	2.24
Bill Durnan	1943–50	7	383	22,945	901	34	2.36
Jacques Plante	1952–63	18	837	49,533	1,965	82	2.38
Patrick Roy	1984–95	13	652	37,920	1,722	37	2.72
Georges Vezina	1917–26	9	191	11,564	633	13	3.28

SEA=Seasons with Canadiens   MIN=Minutes Played   GAA=Goals Against Average
YRS=Years in the NHL   GA=Goals Against
GAMES=Games Played   SH=Shutouts

The Montreal Canadiens Hockey Team

CHAPTER NOTES

Chapter 1

1. Ross Renne, *Montreal Canadiens* (Mankato, Minn.: Creative Education, Inc., 1990), p. 13.
2. Stan and Shirley Fischler, *Great Book of Hockey* (Lincolnwood, Ill.: Publications International, Ltd., 1996), p. 126.
3. Brian McFarlane, *Stanley Cup Fever* (Toronto: Stoddart Publishing Co. Limited, 1992), p. 117.
4. Ibid.
5. Renne, p. 14.

Chapter 2

1. Kevin Allen, "Notes: National Hockey League," *USA Today*, March 12, 1996, p. 5C.
2. Stan and Shirley Fischler, *Great Book of Hockey* (Lincolnwood, Ill.: Publications International, Ltd., 1996), pp. 235–236.

Chapter 3

1. Zander Hollander, ed., *The Complete Encyclopedia of Hockey* (Detroit: Visible Ink Press, 1993), p. 199.
2. Ibid.
3. Ibid., p. 200.
4. Ibid.
5. Stan and Shirley Fischler, Morgan Hughes, Joseph Romain, and James Duplacey, *20th Century Hockey Chronicle* (Lincolnwood, Ill.: Publications International, Ltd., 1994), p. 226.
6. Ibid., p. 214.
7. Jonathan Bliss, *The Centers* (Vero Beach, Fla.: Rourke Book Company, Inc., 1994), p. 17.
8. Fischlers, et. al., p. 214.
9. Dan Diamond and Joseph Romain, *Hockey Hall of Fame* (Toronto: Doubleday Canada Limited, 1988), p. 94.
10. Jay Greenberg, Frank Orr, and Gary Ronberg, *NHL: The World of Professional Ice Hockey* (New York: The Rutledge Press, 1981), p. 224.
11. Ibid.
12. E. M. Swift, "Saving Grace," *Sports Illustrated*, June 21, 1993, p. 27.

Chapter 4

1. Gary Ronberg, *The Hockey Encyclopedia* (New York: Macmillan Publishing Co., Inc., 1974), p. 194.

2. Stan Fischler, *Coaches* (Toronto: Warwick Publishing Inc., 1995), p. 37.

3. Stan and Shirley Fischler, Morgan Hughes, Joseph Romain, and James Duplacey, *20th Century Hockey Chronicle* (Lincolnwood, Ill.: Publications International, Ltd., 1994), p. 378.

4. Fischler, p. 42.

5. E. M. Swift, "Super Conductor," *Sports Illustrated*, May 10, 1993, p. 60.

Chapter 5

1. Stan and Shirley Fischler, Morgan Hughes, Joseph Romain, and James Duplacey, *20th Century Hockey Chronicle* (Lincolnwood, Ill.: Publications International, Ltd., 1994), p. 82.

2. Brian McFarlane, *Stanley Cup Fever* (Toronto: Stoddart Publishing Co. Limited, 1992), p. 71.

3. Fischlers, et. al., p. 154.

4. McFarlane, p. 128.

5. Ibid., p. 136.

6. Ibid., p. 156.

7. Fischlers, et. al., p. 378.

8. Ibid.

Chapter 6

1. Eric Duhatschek, *1994 Information Please Sports Almanac* (Wilmington, Mass.: Houghton Mifflin Company, 1994), p. 347.

2. E. M. Swift, "Saving Grace," *Sports Illustrated*, June 21, 1993, p. 31.

The Montreal Canadiens Hockey Team

GLOSSARY

blue lines—The two lines on the ice that mark the beginning of the offensive zones.

Calder Trophy—Presented annually to the NHL's Rookie of the Year.

face-off—A method in which two opponents attempt to gain control of the puck, which is dropped by the referee.

"Flying Frenchmen"—Traditional nickname of the Canadiens, who historically are known for their great skating ability and their French heritage.

goalmouth—The area directly in front of the goal.

goals-against average (GAA)—The average number of goals a goaltender allows per game.

Hart Trophy—Presented annually to the NHL's Most Valuable Player.

hat trick—Three or more goals in a game scored by one player.

Les Habitants (*Les Habs*)—A common nickname of the Canadiens. It is French for "the inhabitants."

penalty box—The area where a penalized player sits until his penalty is over.

points (player)—A player's total number of goals and assists.

points (team)—A team earns two points for a win and one for a tie.

power play—A situation in which one team temporarily has an extra player (or players) on the ice because of a penalty on the other team.

red line—The center line on the ice.

slap shot—A hard shot in which the shooter brings his stick way back and then slaps at the puck.

Stanley Cup—Presented annually to the NHL's championship team.

Sudden death—The overtime period (or periods). The first team to score first wins.

Vezina Trophy—Presented annually to the NHL's best goalie, named for the Canadiens' Georges Vezina.

FURTHER READING

Diamond, Dan, ed. *The Official National Hockey League 75th Anniversary Commemorative Book.* Toronto: McClelland & Stewart Inc., 1991.

Fischler, Stan and Shirley, Morgan Hughes, Joseph Romain, and James Duplacey. *20th Century Hockey Chronicle.* Lincolnwood, Ill.: Publications International, Ltd., 1994.

Hollander, Zander, ed. *The Complete Encyclopedia of Hockey.* Detroit: Visible Ink Press, 1993.

Joseph, Paul. *Hockey.* Minneapolis: Abdo & Daughters, 1996.

Knapp, Ron. *Top 10 Hockey Scorers.* Springfield, N.J.: Enslow Publishers, Inc., 1994.

McFarlane, Brian. *Hockey for Kids.* New York: Morrow Junior Books, 1996.

Renne, Ross. *Montreal Canadiens.* Mankato, Minn.: Creative Education, Inc., 1990.

Rockwell, Bart. *World's Strangest Hockey Stories.* Watermill Press, 1993.

Romain, Joseph and James Duplacey. *Hockey Superstars.* Greenwich, Conn.: Brompton Books Corp., 1994.

INDEX

WHERE TO WRITE

Montreal Canadiens
Centre Molson
1260 de La Gauchetiere St. W.
Montreal, Quebec H3B 5E8

WEBSITE

http://www.nhl.com/teampage/mon